CREATING
ZERO-
INCIDENT
CULTURE

Getting employees to *work safely*
when management is not around

MODELING

COACHING

ENGAGING

KEITH BARDNEY

CREATING A
ZERO-INCIDENT
CULTURE

Getting employees to work safely when management is not around

Printed in the United States of America
ISBN: 978-1977699640

Credits

Editor	Brenda Quinn, Writer and Editor, Frisco, TX
	brendalquinn@gmail.com
Copy Editor	Kathleen Green, Positively Proofed, Plano, TX
	info@PositivelyProofed.com
Design, Art Direction, and Production	Melissa Farr, Back Porch Creative, Frisco, TX
	info@BackPorchCreative.com

"Keith is the true definition of servant leadership. This trait has helped him transform cultures, attitudes, and results. Because of his strength in connecting passion, people, and results, he has had an outstanding career in driving safety performance and productivity. Keith is a leader who walks the talk and goes beyond the standard to help people achieve world-class excellence. His dynamic personality will jump out and grab you and challenge your thought process on how you can be effective through engagement, influence, and leadership."

> – Rudy Quick,
> Plant Manager, Blue Apron

"To change the overall safety culture of an organization at all levels, you need a transformational leader with the skill set, knowledge, and compassion to execute a plan. Keith Bardney is able to engage technicians on the floor, empower frontline leaders, and garner support from senior management to create a safe working environment."

> – Dirrek Moore,
> Engineering Manager, Blue Apron

"The greatest part of the 'Bardney Coaching' technique is when a new leader learns how easily trust can be earned with positivity in the first meeting. Whether it is a one-on-one or a group session, Keith's positivity is contagious."

> – Wayne Waite,
> Safety Consultant

"Keith is a strong, skillful, persuasive speaker who gets everyone, from upper management to line employees, to believe that the task is doable. Keith's approach is a true example of what camaraderie is all about."

> – John Raggio,
> Plant Manager, Kraft Heinz

"Keith's unique ability to quickly identify the strengths, weaknesses, and gaps in a facility's processes and safety culture allows him to formulate a practical and doable plan."
— Dana Lewis,
Retired Safety & Health Director

"Keith always has a smile on his face, listens intently to everyone's point of view, and provides a great example of how a world-class safety professional carries himself. I strive to emulate his leadership style every day and will always value his mentorship."
— Darren Austin,
Vice President/Senior Risk Consultant,
HUB International

"Keith is extremely knowledgeable about safety and a strong presenter who drives engagement with his audience to achieve lasting results."
— Victor Delgado,
President, Dale Carnegie of New Mexico/
El Paso, Texas/Stockton and Modesto, California

"Both as a safety leader and as a personal coach/mentor, Keith exceeded the standard and showed what makes him an outstanding leader who produces high-impact results. He takes the time to get to know teams and individuals and ensures that he is helping create a culture that engages, empowers, and develops other leaders"
— Mike Alston Jr.,
Associate Director, Engineering & Facilities,
Sterogene Bioseparations, Inc.

Dedication

This book is dedicated to my wife, Yulonda. It would never have been written without her love and support. When I was asked to write a book about what I'd taught for so many years, I knew I needed her assistance to make this a reality. She happily agreed and her contributions and advice shaped the development of this book.

Contents

Foreword

As the platform safety director over at a large food manufacturing company, I can only attempt to describe the significance of Keith's leadership coaching, or "the Bardney Leadership Coaching," as we call it.

Keith conducted the first plant implementation training at our company in 2013 and immediately established leadership buy-in and understanding. That first day, Keith personally taught the technique as he worked side by side with the plant manager, and in no time the plant manager was teaching the technique to new supervisors.

Keith carried on and repeated this training on every shift in each of our twenty facilities. I can attest that he personally taught floor supervisors one-on-one in all but one location.

Keith recognized that this leadership approach was a gift he'd received from others, and he felt compelled to develop it and teach it to (or pour it into) others personally, rather than just send out an email or directive.

Our supervisors were often new to leadership, and Keith gave them a tool that allowed them to coach others in a way that ensured employees changed their behavior for their own safety, and not because their supervisors were watching. This training inspired a wide range of coaching events: leader to employee, peer to peer, and even worker to supervisor (although we determined that coaching of spouses or significant others should not be attempted!). Through these coaching events, the safety culture changed from finding blame to holding pre-shift discussions about the best way to recognize individuals and make further improvements.

That first plant cut its incident rate in half in the first six months, and in half again by the following fiscal year. Our platform results have dropped to one-third of that initial rate. Even more significant is the fact that our culture is more focused on working together to ensure everyone goes home the same way they came to work.

Whenever Keith comes to visit our plants, he is always welcomed by the operations supervisors, who challenge him to walk in their work areas for fifteen minutes and find someone doing a task unsafely. Thanks to Keith's coaching, the supervisors are now confident that their teams are working safely, whether or not the supervisors are on the floor. And Keith is always welcome to come and visit.

– Tony Campbell,
Director of Safety

Introduction

Creating a Zero-Incident Culture presents a new twist on developing a sustainable safety process in a manufacturing environment. Quite simply, it's about my endeavor to keep employees out of the hospital. My desire is to see each and every employee go home to their families the way each one of them came to work: alive and with all their limbs. So I developed an approach to safety that's simple, straightforward, costs nothing, saves companies millions of dollars, and has been proven to work in various industries. The system is realistic and so easy to implement that anyone can do it.

My approach to safety started with developing a foundation. I established that foundation with my first coach/mentor, built on it as I learned from many influential safety leaders, and still use it today. Back in the early 1980s there wasn't much of a safety process to duplicate, so I adapted many of the initial elements from a quality process.

As you read through each chapter, you'll see how I continue to draw on that foundation I set early in my career. It was working...why change it? I essentially do the same things today; however, I do them with much more focus. If you have a good foundation, don't throw it out for every new system that comes along. Tweak your existing process to focus your activities and bring greater value to what you do. Do what works and just fine-tune one or two aspects that will help you become a more effective safety professional. I like to keep things simple; if it's too complicated, I won't do it, the employees won't do it, and you probably won't do it, either.

Safety is a people business. Make sure you engage people from all levels of the organization in the safety process. Without their involvement, you will work much too hard and find yourself frustrated and perplexed as to why people continue to work unsafely despite the accidents, injuries, and sometimes even deaths happening around them. People are spontaneous, emotional, and unpredictable at times. How do you contain those human tendencies in a busy manufacturing environment with so many moving parts? I show you how to get people to do what's in their best interest through influence and effective leadership.

Throughout this book, you'll learn about my approach to safety through a series of real-life anecdotes from the past twenty-eight years that explain my understanding of safety. You can follow along with my reasoning and the decisions that were made. I like to add a bit of levity to all situations because safety can be kind of dry and boring. My hope is that you'll see yourself in me and realize that if a guy like me can do this, despite all the mistakes I made, surely you can do it, too.

I wish you success as you drive your organization toward safety excellence.

chapter one

The Cost of
Doing Business

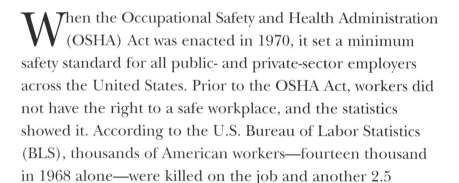

When the Occupational Safety and Health Administration (OSHA) Act was enacted in 1970, it set a minimum safety standard for all public- and private-sector employers across the United States. Prior to the OSHA Act, workers did not have the right to a safe workplace, and the statistics showed it. According to the U.S. Bureau of Labor Statistics (BLS), thousands of American workers—fourteen thousand in 1968 alone—were killed on the job and another 2.5 million workers suffered a disabling disease or an injury.

I started working for Company #1 in 1984, fourteen years after OSHA became law, yet we still hadn't figured out how to prevent workers from getting injured. BLS reported that in 1984, 5.4 million workers suffered a disabling disease or an injury on the job. Could it be that, in spite of the law, the following scenarios that I witnessed were also happening in other manufacturing facilities across the country? For example, while I was working as a quality control technician I saw people driving forklift trucks and speeding around corners to get an order out, maintenance people working at elevation without fall protection to get a line going, and hourly employees sticking their hands in moving equipment to unjam product.

These are just a few examples of how the behavior of employees can create an unsafe environment for themselves and others. Yet management did not discourage these unsafe behaviors—and the silence from management sent a strong message that unsafe behaviors were acceptable and, therefore, it was up to the employees to not get hurt.

At Company #1, we met the minimum OSHA requirements, but we didn't have a safety management system in place at the time. Basically, we were reactive, and Human Resources (HR) administered the injury investigations. HR filled out the accident reports, sent employees to the hospital, submitted claims to the workers' compensation insurance carrier, wrote very basic safety rules, and conducted safety orientations. That was the full extent of our safety process. The focus was on following policies and procedures and complying with federal and state regulations.

This was the typical way to handle safety on the job in the late 1980s and early 1990s. Injuries were acceptable since employees were expected to meet production quotas at all costs, workers' compensation costs were just another business expense, and safety was not a part of the annual business plan. The safety professional, commonly called the "safety cop," was solely responsible for carrying out the company safety processes and performed intermittent inspections alone. Safety processes were reactive, and employees worked safely only when management was around. At Company #1, for example, I often observed that when management was out on the production floor, employees adjusted personal protective equipment (PPE), adjusted their lifting posture, and locked out equipment within the first two or three minutes of walking into their areas.

These are typical characteristics of what I call the Dependent Stage of a safety process, so named because employees are dependent on management to enforce the safety rules. At this stage of a safety process, employees often don't work safely unless management is present. Safety processes like these were the standard in the 1980s and 1990s, and they still exist today.

FIGURE 1.

DEPENDENT STAGE
Employees rely on management for their safety

Safety is focused on technical and procedural solutions and compliance with regulations.

Safety is not considered a key business risk.

Safety manager is perceived as having primary responsibility for safety.

Many accidents are considered unavoidable because accidents are just the cost of doing business.

Most frontline supervisors are focused on production, not safety.

Safety processes are reactive and consist mostly of incident investigations.

> The only measurements of the safety process are lost-time rates.
>
> Accident rates are worse than the industry average.
>
> Hourly employees follow policy and procedures because they are told to do so.
>
> Management's responsibility is to give orders and employees' responsibility is to do what they are told.
>
> Management style is command and control.
>
> Safety incentives, such as cash or prizes, are offered as a way to reduce lost-time and recordable incidents.

At the Dependent Stage of any safety process, accidents are seen as unavoidable and are simply considered the cost of doing business. Working safely is said to be a priority—until the company's priorities change—and when there are injuries, well, that's the employees' fault. Today, most employers have comprehensive OSHA compliance processes in place, and a few safety processes go much further than the basics, but many of those attitudes about employee responsibility and accountability still exist.

chapter two

Command and Control

After a year in quality control and two years in research and development at Company #1, I asked to be transferred to production to learn how to manage people and processes. I knew that experiencing the pressures of a fast-paced environment and managing employee behaviors would benefit me when I got into safety.

My career in production began in the English muffins department. I'm a very goal-oriented person, and in those days nothing was going to keep me from hitting my production numbers. Our production quota was 75 percent and I'm proud to say I consistently hit 82 percent.

The predominant leadership style in that era was command and control. That's how my supervisors had handled their teams and, naturally, I adopted that approach when I became a production supervisor. If you've never had the pleasure of working for someone who uses the command-and-control approach, it looks like this: The boss is totally in charge and everybody knows it. The boss is always banging a fist on the table, barking orders, screaming at you when you screw up, and blaming you and everyone else when things go wrong. The boss says nothing when you perform well, of course, barely speaks to or acknowledges you at the start of the shift, and never has a kind word to say.

Yep, that was me. I had been taught that employees are not your friends, so do not build relationships with them. Do not smile or joke with them. Treat each employee like a number, not a person. Do not show your soft side; look mean at all times and threaten to fire them when they don't perform well, call in sick, or don't follow your orders. This was the kind of atmosphere I created for my employees in production. Although I consistently hit 82 percent of my production quota, it often came at the emotional expense of my employees.

My team in the English muffins department consisted of seventeen employees who reported directly to me. And, based on their job performance, I "racked and stacked" them from top to bottom. Leaders rarely acknowledge doing this, but it's common practice.

My #1 employee was Julian, a workhorse who I hoped would never call in sick or take vacation. When Julian came to work, life was great. Julian set up for production, he gave breaks to team members, fixed broken-down equipment, and helped solve day-to-day issues. No matter what I needed, Julian took care of it with a sense of urgency, usually exceeding my expectations.

When Julian called in sick, however, life turned south for me because I had to work like a dog to do everything Julian did. He made my job easier, but of course I never thanked him or spoke words of encouragement to show my appreciation.

Now, I don't know how safely Julian performed his tasks, nor did I care. I had a production goal to meet and I was only concerned with hitting my numbers. As long as Julian got the job done, whatever he did was fine with me.

And then there was my #17 person: Oscar. Let's just say that whatever Julian was, Oscar wasn't. He was by far the least productive employee on my team. I prayed he would call in sick more often or just quit. Whenever I saw Oscar getting out of his car in the parking lot, I visualized my production going down—and he hadn't even punched in yet. When I gave Oscar a job to do, it was the absolute opposite of giving Julian a job to do. It would take Oscar three times longer than it should have to complete a task, and he usually did it wrong.

As a command-and-control leader, I just wanted Oscar to follow my orders and do the job correctly. I didn't care if the work wasn't done safely. I often caught Oscar doing something wrong and, trust me, I let him know it every time. I would actually walk past employees doing their jobs correctly to get to that one person, usually Oscar, doing the job incorrectly. I would scream and holler at him. I would threaten to fire him or put him on oddball jobs.

One day, we had a truck waiting on product when, as luck would have it, production suddenly stopped. I know you're familiar with Murphy's Law, which states that whatever can go wrong does go wrong, and always at the worst possible time.

Well, this was one of those worst possible times. Back in the eighties, a truck would wait for product for only two hours and then would leave, even if it had only a partial load. That was a very costly mistake, and if that happened, you were subject to being terminated.

On this day in 1987, production had stopped and the English muffins were piling up on the cooling conveyor while the truck waited. So I got on the intercom and hollered at Oscar to come to the production office. Yes, I actually called #17 Oscar. Surely this was Murphy's Law at work once again, but Oscar was trained in, familiar with, and responsible for the operation of the cooling conveyor in the packaging area. I didn't have high hopes.

As a backup plan, I then called maintenance on the intercom to get that line going. However, I knew it would take maintenance fifteen to thirty minutes just to show up, so unfortunately I was pretty much depending on Oscar.

As soon as Oscar got to the office, I yelled at him: "Get that cooling conveyor line going!" Given the urgency, I know the tone of my voice communicated to Oscar, "Do whatever it takes!" to get that line back in operation.

So Oscar took off running across the floor, which was oily and covered with muffin dough. Oscar definitely had a slip, trip, and fall risk here. Next, Oscar went climbing onto the packaging equipment, with no fall protection and no ladder, to reach the conveyor located fifteen feet up from the floor. He could have easily slipped and fallen during his climb. Then, fifteen feet in the air, Oscar lay face down, spread-eagle, untangling the wire-mesh conveyor. He could have fallen off the conveyor. And finally, he didn't take the time to lock out the equipment as he stuck his fingers into the conveyor to remove muffins that were stuck. After the cooling conveyor was cleared out, it could have easily started up again, mangling or even severing Oscar's hands and fingers. Oscar's risks that day were probably a 9 on a scale of 1 to 10.

Did I tell Oscar to do all these unsafe things? Verbally, I did not, but I might as well have since I didn't stop him. When a supervisor does not stop an employee from doing something unsafe, the supervisor has just said that the employee's actions are acceptable.

On that day in 1987, all I was concerned about was that Oscar had done exactly what I'd ordered him to do—and probably for the first time ever. Reminding him to work safely was the furthest thing from my mind. That was not our culture at the time.

But what would I do today, thirty years later, if given a chance to reenact this situation? I would say something like this: "Oscar, go; the cooling conveyor is down, but walk, don't run, grab a ladder and fall protection, and let me see your lock. Great. Please lock out the cooling conveyor; now go."

The difference between 1987 and today is that today I would give safety instructions to Oscar to reduce his risk tremendously, from a 9 in 1987 to a 2 today. Why not a 0? Well, zero risk does not exist in life. Safety is defined as reducing risk to an acceptable level, and 2 is an acceptable level of risk, in my opinion.

The key here is to raise safety expectations. My expectation for production was very high, but my expectation for quality and safety was very low. What's interesting is that I went to school for safety and started off my career in quality, and yet I had very low expectations for both. Also, I've realized since then that people will meet your minimum expectations. You get what you expect; if you expect much out of people, you will receive much in return.

To my great surprise, within about twenty minutes Oscar had the cooling conveyor running again. I gave him the attaboy look without saying the words. Once again, in the command-and-control era, "thank you" was rarely uttered. We finished the order and got the truck loaded within our two-hour window.

Although I had earned a college degree in occupational safety, for me, production took priority over safety—always. Safety made up probably only 1 percent of who I was at the time, while production made up the other 99 percent, and quality was 0 percent. And because that's who I was, what message did I send to my team about safety in 1987? Probably something like this:

- Safety is important, but only if it doesn't interfere with production.

- You are responsible for your own safety. It's your fault if you perform a task unsafely and get injured.

- You get an attaboy when it comes down to production but no acknowledgment for working safely.

These were all the wrong messages, but they were common back in the 1980s, and they're still common today in the Dependent Stage of a safety culture.

Given the safety culture of Company #1 at that time—combined with multiple unsafe acts by the Oscars of the company 24 hours a day, 365 days a year—it's no surprise that the safety numbers were horrible. The OSHA incident rate (OIR) was 19.8, which essentially meant we were sending 20 out of every 100 people to the hospital. The average OIR in the food industry at the time was 9.2.

Additionally, our workers' compensation experience modification rate (EMR) was 2.2, while the average was 1.0. The EMR is made up of three components: combined salaries, type of industry, and frequency and severity of claims from the previous three years. The only aspect we could impact was the frequency and severity of claims. Our company losses were double those of the average food company and our premiums reflected that. However, the moment we realized that we could impact the rate of injuries, we also reduced claims and quickly saw the savings in the form of lower premiums. Those savings went back to the company and were invested in upgrading operating equipment.

Every so often HR brought in the insurance carrier to talk to the supervisors about safety. I remember being so frustrated because HR had no idea of all the things that I, as a production supervisor, needed to be concerned about: efficiency, yield, wasted ingredients, finished products, employees calling in sick, poor performers, rework, and employee complaints. HR talked as if I had time to be concerned about safety, too. Back then, I figured that if HR wanted to focus on safety, they should hire a safety professional and leave the supervisors alone.

I can vividly remember sitting in one of those meetings when HR and the insurance carrier came in to talk to us and gave us a long laundry list of things we were expected to do. Of course I nodded my head in agreement, as if I were onboard with the whole thing. But when the HR people left, so did that list. I couldn't possibly do all those things—nor was I going to try. My boss didn't put my job on the line when we had accidents, but he did when I didn't hit my production numbers. Back then, in my mind, safety didn't make us money and therefore it wasn't important. Production made us money, so that's all my company cared about—and so did I.

Lessons Learned

○ It's true that safety doesn't make us money, but it saves the money we make. As I say at the plants I visit, if accident prevention (safety) is the only work we do and we produce nothing, we'll go out of business. We must be able to produce a quality product, and we must produce it accident-free.

○ Unsafe acts will occur unless you make a conscious effort to correct each and every unsafe act you come across. If you see unsafe acts, as I saw Oscar doing, and don't address them, you're communicating that it's okay to act that way.

○ People will meet your minimum expectations. If your expectations are low, your employees will perform at a low level. In the eighties, my expectations for production were high but my expectations for safety and quality were non-existent. When I later raised my expectations for safety and quality, employees met those expectations, and production remained high as well.

○ In the eighties, we expected employees to get injured as a cost of doing business, and you get what you expect. As a result of that thinking, our company losses were double those of the average food company, and our sky-high premiums reflected that. But when we changed our thinking and realized that reducing injuries would lower both our claims and our premiums, we were able to invest the savings in upgrading operating equipment.

chapter three

Safety is a Priority

By the late 1980s, Company #1 had one of the worst safety records in the food industry. People fell off platforms, slipped on wet surfaces, got struck by moving objects, and had to perform unbelievable acrobatic acts just to get product out the door. Finally, in 1989, Company #1 decided to create a position for a safety coordinator.

I had spent two years in production, so I understood how many of these unsafe acts could have happened. Of course, as a floor supervisor driven by production goals, I didn't see safety issues as my problem. But I'd gone to college for occupational safety and I always figured that I would work in this field at some point, so I was willing to give it a try. I applied for the position.

I remember the interview clearly, as if it happened just yesterday.

Terry, in his deep Southern voice, opened the interview like this: "Bardney, I'm looking for a corporate safety coordinator. I heard you were good with production."

Of course I was excited, but I just nodded and smiled. Inside, I was busting. I could barely contain my enthusiasm. *Yep, that's me!* I said to myself.

"I heard you were good with getting results," he drawled.

I smiled and nodded some more. "Yes, I've had good results," I said, trying to stay cool. Inside, I was proudly sticking out my chest. *You know it! Keep on talking, buddy!*

"But there's one thing about you that worries me, Bardney," he added, his tone of voice becoming more forceful.

What? My chest deflated just a bit. *What was he talking about?*

"I was told you were terrible with people."

Now, those were fighting words where I come from. Inside, I already had my fists up, ready for a fight. I knew exactly where Terry got that feedback. It could only have come from one person: our HR representative. I'm sure her comments were based on the number of employees coming up to her office complaining about me every week.

But all Terry said was this: "So I'm going to show you how to deal with and work with people," and moved on to his next question.

At the end of the interview, Terry said that there are two important groups when it comes to manufacturing: the group that sells our products and the group that makes our products. From a safety standpoint, I couldn't do much for the group that sells our products because I wouldn't see them much. But I could do a lot for the group making our products.

"As a matter of fact, Bardney," he said, "it's important to remember that you and other managers don't make the products. The people on the production floor are the ones doing all the work, so you need to treat them like kings and queens. You'll become successful only if you help them be successful, by giving them the knowledge they need, getting their input, and following up on their recommendations."

I later came to know this approach as a servant style of leadership. Up until this time, all I knew was a command-and-control environment in which the boss was king.

Despite the rough patch in the interview, I got the safety coordinator job. From that point on, because I had the privilege of working with Terry, everything I knew about managing people and processes changed for the better, thanks to Terry's coaching and the high bar he set. I fundamentally changed my thinking and my approach to my own role as a leader. I had a lot of bad habits to overcome, though, and it took me nearly two years to fully wrap my head around the servant style of leadership.

Terry was not only my manager but also my mentor. As the vice president of Total Quality Management (TQM), he was responsible for quality systems, food safety, sanitation, and employee safety throughout the company.

My first few months in the job were busy and sometimes chaotic and showed just how new we were to safety, how much we needed to learn, and how unprepared we were for what might happen.

In my very first week on the job, I learned my toughest safety lesson ever. An employee was working inside the auger, a conveyor that moves food product from processing to packaging. He should have locked out the equipment, but he didn't, so that was safety issue #1. Safety issue #2 was related to the design of the equipment: it was easier to turn on than to turn off. For safety purposes, the prominent, easily accessible mushroom-head button should have been on the red stop button, making it easy to shut down the equipment in an emergency, and the green start button should have been recessed so that an accidental bump would not start the equipment. But, unfortunately, the equipment had not been designed that way. And so, as the employee was cleaning the auger, he bumped against the mushroom-head start button and the auger blades amputated three of his fingers.

I was sitting fifty feet away, so I heard the screams. I immediately ran over to help—but, to be honest, I didn't know what to do! I'd been the safety coordinator for less than a week and we had not yet put an emergency process in place.

So I started running around trying to figure out what to do. I yelled for someone to call for medical assistance, and then all I could do was pick up the amputated fingers and put them in a plastic bag.

Life for that employee and his family was forever altered that day. And my life was changed, too. It was my first experience with an injury that devastating, and I vowed it would be my last. I never want to see anything like that again.

This event raised a sense of urgency in me and set the stage to make safety an integral part of what we do every day. But that would happen only if we made fundamental changes to the safety culture at Company #1. Safety would no longer be ignored, overlooked, or put on the back burner.

From that day forward, operations started off every shift in a huddle meeting talking about injuries from the previous day, pointing out unsafe conditions to look out for, and recognizing the number of days without a lost-time injury.

Terry taught me how to lead teams to drive safety performance by creating a vision, a strategy, an action plan, and a series of metrics. Within weeks we began to shift the culture, transitioning from our reactive approach to a proactive approach, as follows:

> **Vision:** Safety was such an integral part of what we did that Terry taught us to think world-class safety and to benchmark against the best (safest) companies, not just in the food industry but in all industries.
>
> I remember him gathering the senior leadership team and talking about where we were (OIR of 19.8) and how far we needed to go for our safety performance to be considered world-class (OIR of 2.0 or less). Terry said we needed to update existing policies and procedures, develop a comprehensive audit system, form strong safety committees, implement suggestion boxes, and create a special maintenance task force to fix all of the conditions

brought to our attention by the safety committees and suggestion boxes.

Strategy: Safety was such an integral part of what we did that Terry taught me, as well as the safety committee, how to strategize so that we could take the organization to world-class safety performance. He encouraged us to analyze where our injuries were coming from and brainstorm ideas to reduce injury risks. Terry also taught us how to assess the production plants to determine what compliance gaps we had and how to get into compliance. The overall strategy was to keep employees out of the hospital by making sure we were always in OSHA compliance.

Action Plans: Safety was such an integral part of what we did that Terry taught me how to bring together both the operations team and the hourly employees in safety committees, and work with them to develop impactful action plans to drive our strategy.

These action plans included activities to reduce our top three loss sources: trips, slips, and falls; struck-by and struck-against injuries; and material-handling injuries. These action plans also included auditing all high-risk areas and training all employees on job safety and job hazard analyses.

Metrics: Safety was such an integral part of what we did that Terry taught us which key indicators to measure to ensure we were hitting our targets. These metrics primarily consisted of OSHA recordable incidents, lost-time injuries, and workers' compensation (WC) dollars. These were typical measurements of a 1990s compliance-driven safety process, and they're still in use today for safety processes in the Dependent Stage.

The makings of a solid safety process were underway.

Terry demonstrated how to treat our internal customers (our employees) with respect and dignity. This was completely different from the command-and-control approach I'd learned from all other managers in my five-year career. Terry firmly believed in serving our internal customers by training and developing them, asking for their input before making changes, and giving them the tools to do their jobs.

I could not have asked for a better mentor, leader, or coach. Terry was way ahead of his time in his approach to safety leadership and the need to establish a proactive safety culture. He changed my thinking about my role as a leader and helped me get the best from my people.

In year one (1990), by implementing all the activities outlined above, we lowered the OIR to less than 10. That same year, I attended outside training seminars and conferences in safety and TQM, studied leadership books, and received one-on-one coaching from Terry on how to be more proactive in my safety approach.

We called this proactive management approach the Top 10 Elements of a Successful Safety Process, which included:

1. OSHA compliance

2. Management commitment

3. Employee involvement through safety committees

4. Monthly safety training

5. Hazard identification

6. Daily and weekly safety meetings

7. Goal setting and action planning

8. Workers' compensation management

9. Incident investigation

10. Behavior observation

In year two (1991), we brought our OIR down to 6.2, a 69 percent reduction in just two years. We did this by starting to build trust with our hourly associates and fine-tuning the Top 10 Elements. The trust building included doing what we said we were going to do, fixing unsafe conditions, and not accusing employees of deliberately doing something unsafe.

We were clicking on all cylinders—and the best part was that we were keeping more people out of the hospital. This was the year that I received the Employee of the Year award and got promoted to safety manager.

In year three (1992), we brought our OIR down to 4.1 by continuing the successful things we had done in years one and two, and by giving the safety committee more power to act on safety issues. Prior to this, the safety committee would simply give management a list of things to do and walk away with no responsibility. This was the year that we asked safety committee members to propose two possible solutions for each issue they brought up. We also asked them to initiate the corrective actions. We announced this new approach to the entire organization through employee town hall meetings.

In 1993, Terry moved on to another chapter in his career, but through his guidance over the years, he had helped build my confidence and had poured so much knowledge into me that I knew I could carry on in his absence. The OIR was at 2.6 when Terry left the company.

For the next six months, the OIR remained relatively flat. I couldn't understand it. Yes, Terry had left, but why did that mean we couldn't reduce the OIR any further? I was beginning to doubt whether I could do this on my own. I wanted to prove to myself that I could help this company reach world-class safety status, which was still defined as an OIR of 2.0 or less. More than anything, however, I wanted to show Terry that his teaching, coaching, and leadership support hadn't been wasted on me.

I invested six months in working alongside employees on all three shifts, engaging them in conversation in order to build relationships, and asking what they needed to do their jobs better. To my dismay, I discovered that employees were taking unnecessary risks. No one had asked them to; they were just doing whatever they could to keep the production lines running, even if that meant getting injured. This brought back echoes of my own experience as a production supervisor several years before. We needed to change that mindset.

DuPont's Safety Training Observation Program (STOP) was the addition that our process needed. STOP is an award-winning program that DuPont began in the 1980s to increase safety awareness and help people talk to each other about safety every day. STOP focuses on increasing workers' safety awareness, correcting unsafe acts, and coaching employees to help them understand the risks they take. Supervisors are trained to acknowledge the safe acts and correct the unsafe acts they observe.

After introducing STOP into our safety training at Company #1, we continued to make steady improvement. By 1995, the OIR was reduced to 0.9. We had arrived at world-class safety status.

In 1995, I decided to leave the organization and test my safety practices with an aggressive insurance carrier located in the western suburbs of Chicago. I serviced the accounts by coaching them with accident-prevention advice. These companies were in many diverse industries: food, steel (forging), aluminum, die setting, healthcare, textiles, metal plating, and chemical.

This experience with the insurance company benefited me in many ways and taught me:

○ How to dream big and have a huge vision. This organization's vision was to create a zero-accident culture in which every injury could have and should have been prevented. If an injury does occur, it should be treated as if it's the last one the company will ever see. In this zero-accident culture, employees look out for themselves and their fellow employees.

○ How to take accident prevention to another level by focusing on risk instead of just compliance.

○ How to quantify results through laser-focused activities based on the top three loss sources. I learned this approach from my colleague Allen, who challenged me one day while we were reviewing the details of an account with a miserable record of safety performance. His challenge to me was this: "Why are you working on these areas in a broad-brush manner when the area of opportunity is over here?"

I would like to pause here for a minute. As a college student and a young safety professional, I was taught to go into a plant and conduct inspections, comply with governmental regulations and company policy and procedures, and work on broad-brush, feel-good things. The laser-focused approach that I learned during my tenure at the insurance company was the total opposite of everything I'd been taught, but it was a powerful tool that helped bring about real change.

This focused approach involves looking at the top three losses and forming specific action plans to mitigate the risk. This approach is definitely not taught in colleges, nor is it taught by the average manufacturing company. Later in my career, it was this skill set that enabled me to take a safety process to another level and reach the Independent Stage.

Lessons Learned

○ Management is both responsible for and accountable for safety. We expect employees to work safely at all times, but it all starts with management, which is responsible for providing a safe workplace, training employees, and giving them the tools necessary to do their jobs. This was an important lesson from the devastating accident in my first days of my first job in safety. Proper training for that employee might have changed everything.

○ Loss sources must be analyzed in order to impact them. In safety, you can find yourself working on too many general items. Analyzing where injury losses come from gives you an opportunity to create targeted activities to prevent injuries. I learned this targeted approach in my work at the insurance company, and twenty-two years later it is still one of the most effective ways I've found to reduce and prevent injuries.

○ Safety, just like quality, is a continuous improvement process. You constantly strive for zero defects through prevention. At Company #1, our goal was to achieve world-class safety status. To ensure we reached that goal, we used a continuous improvement strategy to measure and make incremental changes to the safety process.

○ What gets measured gets done. Measure safety activities and you will see tasks being completed. Under Terry's leadership, I learned about using metrics to help us hit our targets, which was an effective approach. Our safety process was compliance-driven, however. We were not measuring leading indicators or things that would prevent injuries; we were measuring things on the action plan.

chapter four

Hourly Employees Make the Difference

In 1999, I took a job as an environmental health and safety (EHS) manager for Company #2, a multi-billion-dollar food manufacturer, and was responsible for one plant in Central California. On day one of my new job, I went to Arizona for the company's annual safety conference involving over 250 employees who worked in various safety and operations roles.

I recall that Wayne, the corporate health and safety director, kicked off the meeting by having everyone stand and announce their name, position, plant or office location, and years with the company. When it was finally my turn, I stood and introduced myself and ended with, "This is my first day on the job."

From the attendees seated near me, I learned that this was the first time a new hire had attended an annual safety conference before starting work in a facility. At the time, I didn't understand what the big deal was, but I soon found out. Later that day, during one of the presentations, there it was up on the big screen: a slide listing all fifty of the company's plants by OIR, from best to worst.

At first I didn't see where my new plant ranked since I didn't have my glasses on, but I was sitting next to my plant manager, Tom, so I softly nudged him and whispered, "Where are we on that list?" I don't know if Tom was ignoring me or if he was just really interested in what Wayne was saying, but he sat there in stone-cold silence, just squinting intently at the screen.

So, I finally put on my glasses and looked up at the screen. Can you guess where my plant ranked? Yep, we were down at the bottom at #50, with an OIR of 21.0. At the top of the list, the #1 plant had an OIR of 1.5, while the corporation's overall OIR was 2.6.

I was shocked. We were last? What do you have to do to be last? You can be last without doing anything! We were the Oscar of the organization. I was so annoyed with Tom. He should have told me all of this to prepare me for this conference. This was an embarrassing way to find out how much trouble my new plant was in.

A guy seated near me leaned over. "You're either really, really stupid to take on a plant with a terrible safety record, or really, really smart, because there's nowhere to go but up."

From the podium, Wayne called out, "Where's that new guy who started today?"

I timidly raised my hand and he asked me to stand up.

Oh great, I thought as I rose to my feet. *How bad is this going to get? Now I'm getting called out in front of everybody! I didn't have anything to do with this embarrassing OIR, and no one even warned me what I was getting into.*

"You certainly have your work cut out for you," he said sarcastically. "Welcome to the company."

Everybody got a good laugh out of that. My boss, Tom, still had not even glanced my way.

I'd been in the same situation years before with Company #1, which had a similarly awful record of safety performance when I arrived. But in just six years I took that company to world-class safety status—from an OIR of 19.8 to a 0.9. I wasn't afraid of work; I was charged up. I vowed that at the next safety conference our plant would not be last.

Wayne went on with the conference and talked about the organization's accomplishments and disappointments over the past year. That conference was my first meeting with Wayne, and I got to know him well at Company #2. He was an intense character who would challenge anyone when it came to safety. It was obvious to me even at that first conference that Wayne walked, talked, ate, slept, and breathed safety—morning, noon, and night. His vision and passion for safety were second to none.

After the initial shock of finding out our plant was in last place, the rest of the conference was great. I learned a lot about the company's approach to safety, called the 9 Key Elements of Safety, and how it drove performance and compliance. I also learned that Wayne had been one of the architects of the 9 Key Elements of Safety, which had originated at Procter & Gamble in the late 1960s. At the conference, he talked about how every section of the 9 Key Elements has to be led by hourly employees. As Wayne pointed out, was any group more qualified than the employees to talk about corrective actions and propose ideas to improve their workstations?

The 9 Key Elements of Safety consisted of:

1. Employee involvement

2. Goal setting and action planning

3. Planning for safe conditions

4. Compliance

5. Training

6. Job safety analyses

7. Safe practices

8. Performance tracking

9. Behavior observation system

This process looked very similar to the Top 10 Elements of a Successful Safety Process I'd put together at Company #1. The biggest difference between the two processes was that management ran the safety process at Company #1, while hourly employees ran it at Company #2. I'd never heard of an employee-run safety process and I wanted to learn more about it, so I spent the rest of the conference talking to several people about how the plants got the hourly employees involved. These discussions helped me build some very good relationships with my safety colleagues at the company.

One person I got to know well at that conference was Brian, an H&S manager at the plant in Pittsburgh, who happened to be in my same business unit. I spent quite a bit of time with Brian at the conference, learning all I could about the 9 Key Elements system, and he was more than willing to teach me.

Brian had spent three years with the company, and I was amazed at how much he sounded like Wayne. It turned out that Wayne had personally taken Brian under his wing and coached him. Brian told me about the employee-led safety process he'd created at the Pittsburgh plant, and the results he talked about were so remarkable that I couldn't help but wonder if they were really possible, especially from an employee-run process. I was skeptical, to say the least, so I asked Brian if I could visit his plant to see the employee-run safety process in action. We tentatively agreed I'd head to Pittsburgh the first week in November.

After the one-week conference, I went to work at my California plant for the first time and met my leadership team of seven. They were a close-knit team so I knew I had to fit in, and fast, because my first tomato season would be starting soon.

Tomato season was one thing this company had actually told me about when I was hired, and I'd learned that tomato season every year could make or break our plant. The season ran from the end of June through the end of October and accounted for 70 percent of our plant's revenue. During this season, the plant expanded from 150 employees to 400, and they all worked a hundred days straight without any time off. Truckloads of tomatoes arrived every fifteen minutes, on average, and the plant ran at full speed around the clock.

During my first tomato season, with so much at stake, I didn't want to be an outsider. Outsiders in safety become safety cops, which would mean I'd be working the safety process alone. I needed a committed team for us to succeed. So that first day at the plant I spent thirty minutes with each member of the management team, probing for input on how we could keep our employees out of the hospital.

The responses I got told me that the management team didn't think they could impact the injury rate and they didn't want to take any responsibility for safety. Instead, the team was looking for a safety person to run safety for them.

The company's vision for safety, which I'd seen on full display at the Arizona conference just days before, was nowhere to be found in this plant—and that undoubtedly explained the plant's OIR of 21.0 and its last-place safety ranking. All plant personnel had received training in the company's 9 Key Elements of Safety, but the plant was without a champion to drive the safety culture forward.

The safety ideas the management team gave me looked something like this:

- Write employees up and fire a few to make examples of them.

- Put surveillance on them; half the employees are faking injuries.

- Form safety committees on all three shifts to run safety, which would relieve the plant management team of their responsibilities.

- Work all three shifts to see what's really going on.

○ Observe employees and correct their behaviors.

○ Enforce existing policies and procedures.

○ Conduct a bunch of inspections and get things fixed around here.

○ Work with maintenance to complete corrective actions submitted.

This list from the management team also told me that no one on this team believed in this company's five values:

1. Nothing we do is worth getting hurt.

2. All injuries could have and should have been prevented.

3. Working safely is a condition of employment.

4. Safety and health can be managed.

5. Safety and health is everyone's responsibility.

On that first day at work, I asked all seven people on the leadership team, one by one, if they believed we could take this plant to world-class safety performance, which was still defined as an OIR of 2.0 or less. Remember that our plant had been dead last in the company's safety rankings and our OIR at the time was 21.0.

Five of the seven laughed at me. Tom and Libby kept straight faces, but inside I felt like they wanted to laugh, too. One person responded by saying, "I'll be happy if we get our OIR under 15." That blew me away. Heck, we could get under 15 just by saying hi to the hourly employees.

I said to each of them, "If we don't believe we can do it, we won't. If we're comfortable where we're at, we won't be able to do this."

I knew then that I had a lot of influencing to do since it appeared the team was defeated, overwhelmed, and unsure what to do about all of the injuries. So I told each of them about my success at Company #1 and how I had taken that organization from an OIR of 19.8 to less than 1.0 in six years. I just wanted to give them hope and assure them that I knew how to get us there.

The good news was that at Company #2 the hard work had already been done: The right safety culture had been created at the top levels of the company and the right safety management system already existed. At the corporate level, Company #2 considered safety just as important as production, quality, and sales, and a comprehensive, well-thought-out safety process was already in place. At this plant, however, several critical elements were missing, including interest, confidence, and execution. That's where I came in.

My work at Company #1 and the insurance company had taught me that my first priority would be to find out the cause of the top three injury sources—the nature of the injury, cause, source, department, shift, and more—and work with the plant team to prevent those types of injuries. In addition, without even stepping foot on the production floor, I knew there was low-hanging fruit—and that's where we needed to begin.

At the end of my first week, I held a meeting with that same leadership team and shared my assessment of what we needed to do. At the meeting, I first asked each team member to describe his or her biggest day-to-day issue in running the business, then asked how I could help with each of those issues. This was the servant leadership approach that I learned from Terry. I wanted to be a part of the team. I also asked each of them to walk the production floor with me for thirty minutes, once a week. Through these weekly sessions I'd have an opportunity to train each person to identify safe and unsafe behaviors and conditions, while at the same time they would each have an opportunity to teach me the tomato business, which was set to start in just a few weeks.

Over the next several weeks, I took several proactive steps to help this plant start building the safety culture that was already in place at the top levels of the company:

- ○ I identified the top three losses, including the nature of the injury, cause, source, department, shift, and more. I used this information to determine which department I needed to be in, what I should focus on, and which shifts I needed to work.

- ○ I spent time on all three shifts getting to know our employees and learning about their concerns. Over and over again, the employees said their top concern was that management did not care about safety; they cared only about production.

- ○ I taught each salaried supervisor and hourly lead supervisor how to coach employees about safety in one-on-one situations and in shift huddles, and how to audit their own departments. I made plans to start conducting monthly safety training sessions to educate our hourly employees.

○ I brought the leadership team together to train them in the 9 Key Elements, and I gave them homework assignments that they were expected to discuss with me in our biweekly meetings.

○ I stood at the main entrance daily to thank employees for working safely as they left after each shift, and to welcome the incoming shift of employees. I wanted them all to know I was available at all times to hear their concerns.

Within ninety days, the plant saw a dramatic improvement in safety. The plant had begun FY 1999 with an OIR of 21.0, and in June, the start of tomato season, we began executing our plan. By the end of August, the OIR had been reduced 66 percent to 7.2. In the previous year, over the same three-month period the OIR had stood at 18.4.

We were well on our way. We had done what we said we would do and it was working for us. At the end of the tomato season, in early November 1999, we finished strongly with an OIR of 6.4. The leadership team was excited and, after seeing the results of the focused activities, they started to believe that change was possible.

I silently said to myself, *Here we go again.* I was gaining a reputation for being the turnaround guy.

I then headed to Pittsburgh to visit Brian, the H&S manager I'd met at the annual safety conference. I did want to see the employee-run safety process he'd bragged about, but my real reason for visiting was to expose what was really going on there. No way was a safety process that good being run by hourly employees! I needed to see it with my own eyes.

When I got to the plant, I decided to talk to hourly employees right away. You see, I knew management would say what I wanted to hear, but the hourly employees would tell me the truth, no matter how ugly it was. I was looking for dirt and determined to find it.

Brian met me and took me on an overall plant tour, and the entire time I was totally focused on hourly employees. Were they genuinely working safely? I decided I'd assess the first ten employees we came across. Remember, I'd become a master at the techniques I'd learned from DuPont's STOP process, which focuses on correcting unsafe acts and coaching employees to help them understand the risks they take. I was going to put those coaching techniques to great use.

I saw an employee working inside a piece of equipment and asked him, "What could happen to you while you're repairing this piece of equipment?"

"Nothing," he replied. "I have the main disconnect turned off and my lock is on it."

Okay, I said to myself, *one down, nine to go.* I saw another employee driving around and I was sure I'd see unsafe behaviors this time. But as she drove around a blind corner, she slowed down and beeped the horn. *So much for that one. Okay, eight more to go.*

I did this seven more times without observing any unsafe behavior. But I wasn't convinced quite yet—I was confident I'd see something unsafe with the last one. When I came upon an employee unjamming a bottle of product from the equipment, I said to myself, *I got him now.* But he punched the control button to stop the machine, and then used a tool to pull the bottle out of the danger zone.

I asked him, "What could have happened to you by doing the job that way?"

"Very little could happen to me," he said. "The safety committee member in my area did a risk assessment with the team to minimize our chances of getting injured."

Now I was completely convinced the employees were running the safety show. This was safety at the highest level I had seen in my career.

For the balance of my three-day visit, I focused on learning everything I possibly could about the 9 Key Elements approach and its history. As I finished up my visit, I couldn't stop thinking about how to implement the 9 Key Elements by specifically getting employees more involved at my plant.

I returned to the plant very excited and told the leadership team about my experience at the Pittsburgh plant. The next stage was to informally interview employees to see who I could enlist to be on a central safety committee. I wanted ten of our best from all three shifts to give us a great head start.

After two weeks, we finally nailed down the committee. I talked to them about my safety goals for the plant and told them what I'd seen at the Pittsburgh plant. We decided that if they could do it, so could we.

A strong safety committee was born. We held meetings every month to discuss unsafe conditions and acts. I stressed that they had to lead by example. I said, "You can't influence others if you aren't following the safety rules yourselves." They understood that and showed their commitment to safety by wearing PPE, locking out equipment, and following all the safety rules.

We finished FY 1999 with an OIR of 8.1, a dramatic turnaround from the beginning of FY 1999, when the plant OIR had stood at 21.0. In FY 2000, we started tomato season with the safety committee leading the charge and the leadership team supporting them. We slowly but surely got each safety committee member involved with all 9 Key Elements and finished FY 2000 with an OIR of 5.9.

The results in FYs 2001 and 2002 were even more dramatic. During that period, the leadership team and safety committee achieved even greater safety gains by getting the hourly employees involved in taking action. We had started out with ten members on our central safety committee, but so many hourly employees got involved that we enlisted twenty more members for a total of thirty people across all three shifts. With more employees invested in the safety culture, we made huge progress, achieving an OIR of 4.9 in FY 2001 and 4.1 in FY 2002.

We were changing the safety culture of the plant by getting the hourly employees involved and taking action.

Lessons Learned

○ Safety must be a core value, not just a priority. Values generally don't change; values define who you are and what you stand for, while priorities have a tendency to change based on what is important at the time, such as when production is demanded. At Company #2, it was clear from day one that the senior leadership of the company had embraced safety as a value.

○ Despite the safety commitment at the highest levels of Company #2, my plant did not reflect that commitment. There needed to be a safety champion to show the way forward. The safety process is generally more effective when the plant management team is out front, serving as safety champions, and modeling the safety behaviors that employees can emulate.

○ The involvement of hourly employees is the difference between an average safety process and a great safety process. This was one fundamental difference between Company #1, where management ran the safety process, and Company #2, where the hourly employees ran it. Employee-run processes create a better safety culture because employees are more committed to a safety process that will directly affect them, and because employees know the safety risks they face on the job.

○ As a leader, it's important to keep learning and to keep building on your knowledge so you're not continually starting over. Terry taught me everything he knew about safety, providing a solid foundation. In the years since then, I've continued to add to that foundation with knowledge I gained from Wayne and other safety leaders I've worked with, from the insurance company, and from courses I took and books I read.

chapter five

Proofing the System

After helping my Central California facility dramatically turn around its safety process, in early 2003 I was appointed regional safety manager for five plants at Company #2, four in California, and one in Arizona. I was asked to coach four safety coordinators and safety managers while also running another facility in Central California.

Three of these California plants were facing major safety challenges and each required a tailor-made solution. To find the best solution for each plant, I borrowed an approach from the principles of TQM called "mistake-proofing," or inadvertent-error prevention. In proofing a system, the purpose is to eliminate defects by preventing, correcting, or drawing attention to human errors as they occur.

Plant A

Melisa was the safety coordinator at Plant A in Southern California, which had been recently acquired by Company #2. Melisa had come from the hourly ranks, where she'd spent five years in production. She was well respected by the hourly employees and her greatest strength was her ability to connect with employees.

When I took over the regional role, the plant's OIR was sitting at 7.1. Melisa was eager to learn how to lower this rate and better manage the safety process. The overall safety challenge at Plant A was that production was the sole focus and there was little regard for safety, which is typical when an acquired firm doesn't have an established safety culture.

The plant had implemented some safety measures but, similar to the first plant at Company #2 that I'd worked at, there was no one at the plant to be the safety champion to propel the process forward. As a result, other issues had arisen:

○ Management did not enforce safety procedures.

○ The safety manager had not identified the top injury-loss sources.

○ Employees were not involved in the safety process.

○ The existing safety committee was inactive.

In April 2003, I made my first visit to Plant A, located in a beautiful area of the city. From the outside, it looked more like an office complex than a plant. Melisa greeted me, told me how excited she was, and walked me into a gorgeous conference room where I met the plant manager and his entire leadership team. The presence of the entire team was a great first step in showing the plant's commitment to safety.

I told the team about my background and the way I think about safety. I continued the conversation by painting a picture of how things could be at the plant.

"Can you see this plant producing a quality product accident-free?" I said.

Several people nodded in agreement.

"Can you imagine hitting your production efficiencies, hitting your quality requirements, creating little to no rework—and, at the same time, sending employees home safely to their families every…single…day?"

By now they were all nodding their heads in excitement. "Yes, that's exactly what we want," said the plant manager.

Then I talked about how we would take them from an OIR of 7.1 to world-class safety, an OIR of 2.0 or less.

I talked about how people will do what you do, not what you say, and mentioned that because the management team sets the tone for the culture in a plant, all team members must lead by example.

"For starters," I said, "all management team members will have to commit to wearing PPE, following safety rules, addressing unsafe acts, recognizing safe acts, correcting conditions, and following up on employees' concerns. Are you all committed to doing all those things?"

They responded positively and agreed they could do all of that.

Then I turned to the production manager and asked, "How many people are in your group?"

"Uh, I have a total of 201 employees on all three shifts."

"Who's your #1?" I asked.

He seemed flustered and gave me a confused look.

"Allow me to clarify," I said. "I know this is not something we readily admit, but as leaders we do tend to rack and stack our people. When I worked in production, my #1 employee was Julian. When Julian came to work, life was good. Julian solved problems for me and set up the lines for production. If Julian called in sick, I had to work like a dog and life was terrible."

The production manager nodded. "Okay, I get where you're going. My #1 is—"

"Don't mention any names," I said, stopping him in mid-sentence. Everyone laughed. "Just keep that person's name in your head for now. And who is your #201?"

I told them about Oscar, who'd been at the bottom of my team at #17. I described Oscar and how it seemed that our production went down when he came to work. "If he called in sick, I told him he could take two more days off and he didn't need a doctor's note," I added for effect.

The production manager thought for a moment and just smiled. "Yeah, I have a #201."

I continued, telling them how all team members deserve the same respect, whether they're #1 or #201. Oscar deserved to be treated with the same respect that I gave Julian and the others on my team. As a leader, that was my responsibility, and it was my fault that it didn't always happen. "And it was also important for Oscar to hear more than just correction," I said. "He needed to hear positive reinforcement when he did the right things the right way."

I explained how effective a two-way approach is in engaging employees, and how it can be used in addressing safety, quality, and production issues.

I gave a few examples of the approach. "First, there's the positive reinforcement approach, which I want to stress will probably account for 90 percent of your interactions with employees. When you see an employee who's demonstrating safe behavior, I want you to stop and give that person very specific positive feedback on what they're doing correctly."

I listed some examples of positive reinforcement they might give to employees:

○ I appreciate your locking out the equipment.

○ I appreciate your catching that quality problem before it got to our customer.

○ Thanks for changing over the line in thirty minutes ~~when most employees need forty-five minutes.~~

"Then, I want you to follow up that positive reinforcement with a question to the employee," I said. "I want you to ask: 'How can we get others to do it just like you?' After you ask the question, I want you to just be quiet and wait for the employee's response."

I could see by their faces that everyone in the room was intrigued. I explained to them that I'd learned this positive reinforcement technique from Vic, a trainer with Dale Carnegie. Vic had taught a class for me in my previous role, just before I got promoted to the regional safety position, and I immediately adapted his techniques into my safety approach.

Prior to the training with Vic, I'd always thanked employees with general compliments such as, "Great job for working safely." But as I learned from Vic, generic compliments can sound cheesy and meaningless. He taught me the importance of keeping compliments specific because they sound genuine and sincere. And by asking the follow-up question—"How can we get others to do it just like you?"—the employees became more engaged in the conversation and seemed to feel good about doing a task safely. I explained to the group that Vic's techniques helped me take safety to the next level.

As I continued my presentation to the Plant A leadership team, I explained that although 90 percent of their interactions with employees would involve positive reinforcement, the other 10 percent would take the form of a coaching moment. Those interactions would start something like this:

○ I noticed you were not locking out the equipment.

○ I noticed you were accepting product when you should have been placing it on hold and not keeping up with production-line flow.

○ I noticed it took you sixty minutes to change over the

production line, but the allotted time frame is only forty-five minutes.

"Again, follow up right away and ask the employee this: 'What's the worst that can happen if you continue that practice?' Just stay quiet and wait for the response. And then, after they answer that question, ask, 'If you know that, why would you take that risk?' Be quiet again and wait for the response."

The leadership team practiced these techniques as they role-played. I asked them to keep working on these approaches with employees at least once a day for the next thirty days.

Over the next several weeks, I received many positive emails and phone calls from Plant A. Everyone on the leadership team was practicing the two-way techniques and seeing that the approaches really worked. They'd had good feedback from employees, especially for the positive reinforcement.

I was happy to get the employee feedback on the two-way techniques. I instructed Melisa to ask the leadership team to teach these techniques to the salaried supervisors and hourly leads, and have them practice for the next thirty days.

Within sixty days, Plant A started experiencing a noticeable change. Employees were excited to be positively recognized for working safely and they didn't mind being corrected by their supervisors. At the same time, the plant management team began to notice that employees were looking out for themselves, starting to take responsibility for their own safety—and no longer relying on the company to do it for them.

As a result of this positive reinforcement, the safety culture of the plant began to change. When people receive positive feedback for their safe behavior, they are naturally more motivated to continue that behavior and take more responsibility for themselves. Over time, the safety process changes and matures to the Independent Stage. (See Figure 2 on pages 62-63 for a list of qualities of the Independent Stage.)

After sixty days, I returned to Plant A and conducted a question-and-answer segment with them. Here's a sample of the questions I received that day:

Q: Most employees have seen the approach and I think they're tired of it. What do I do now?

A: I recommend that you thank them for production and quality, as well. I also recommend that you thank them for working safely around their top injury risk. This way you're not just thanking them for wearing their PPE. If you try to do that, you'll be out in the plant thanking everyone every minute of the day and not getting any work done. We expect employees to wear their PPE, so meeting this basic requirement is not anything special.

Q: What do I say if I correct an employee and that person asks, "Why are you picking on me?"

A: I believe it's all in the way you correct them.
To answer this question during the Q&A segment, I asked that person to come up front and role-play with me on the spot. I noticed something immediately when we began to role-play—the participant did not use the two-way approach that I'd taught. He said, "Why are you not holding onto the handrail?" His question should have been phrased

this way: "What's the worst that can happen if you do not hold onto the handrail?" Asking an open-ended question allows the opportunity for a great two-way dialogue.

Q: What happens if I use the two-way approach, coach the employee by asking, "What's the worst that can happen?" and then the next day the employee commits the same unsafe act?

A: I suggest that you approach the employee and say the following: "Yesterday we talked and you told me you understood the worst that could happen to you with that unsafe act. But today I see you doing the exact same unsafe act. What's changed from yesterday?" Now, I wouldn't say this in a mean way, but in a soft, caring voice. The typical answer is, "I forgot." So then I'd ask, "Do you have family at home?" Usually the answer is yes. So I'd say, "I don't want you working safely for me but for yourself and your family. Would you do that moving forward?" They typically say yes and then I thank them.

The team was excited and energized to continue with these approaches. I later met with Melisa and recommended the following activities to keep this new safety culture moving in the right direction:

○ Form a handpicked central safety committee with no more than twelve employees.

○ Identify the top three injury losses and start focusing the two-way approaches on those.

○ Ask supervisors to open their meetings by talking about the previous day's safety observations and safety performance.

○ Set up a date for me to come back and start teaching the 9 Key Elements of Safety to all employees.

Melisa said that, within just a few months, the safety culture at Plant A began to change as the vast majority of employees began looking out for themselves in the following ways: doing head-to-toe checks to make sure they were wearing PPE, consistently locking out their equipment without management telling them to do so, beeping horns when coming around corners, using the correct posture when lifting product, cleaning up their areas to prevent slip, trip, and fall hazards, and generally following safe practices. She estimated that 90 percent of the employees were working safely for themselves. These activities were a clear indication that Plant A was now in the Independent Stage of its safety process.

Plant A soon started to see its safety numbers improve, which was exciting since those improvements were the direct result of their focused activities. Plant A had started this process with an OIR of 7.1 and ended FY 2004 with an OIR of 5.0. They continued making progress, ending FY 2005 with a 3.3 and FY 2006 with a 2.2. They were on their way to world-class safety!

Figure 2.

INDEPENDENT STAGE

Employees look out for themselves

Safety is seen as a business risk, and management time and effort is devoted to accident prevention.

Safety focus is on adherence with rules, procedures, and engineering controls.

Accidents are seen as preventable.

Management perceives that the majority of accidents are solely due to the unsafe behavior of frontline staff.

Safety performance is measured with lagging indicators (e.g., injury rates).

Plant management becomes involved in health and safety issues only if accidents increase; punishment is likely to be used.

Accident rates are near or better than the industry-sector average, but accidents tend to be more serious.

Safety is changing from a priority to a value. The emphasis is on individual accountability, management commitment, personal skill building, personal goals, and employee training.

Accident rates are low but have reached a plateau.

Plant staff realizes that employee involvement is essential for safety improvement.

Management recognizes that a wide range of factors lead to accidents, which often stem from management decisions.

A significant proportion of frontline employees are willing to work with management to improve health and safety.

The majority of staff members accept personal responsibility for their own health and safety.

Safety performance is actively monitored and the data used.

Plant B

Al was the EHS manager at Plant B, which produced single-serve condiments and sauces. The plant had approximately 400 employees. He had been with Company #2 for more than twenty-two years as a safety manager at a larger plant, and within the past twelve months had transferred to Plant B. He knew the ins and outs of the 9 Key Elements of Safety process, but he had his hands full with this plant because the culture prioritized production over safety.

Plant B's OIR at the time was 6.5. Its biggest safety issue was Al's command-and-control management style, which was so ingrained in his way of thinking that all he knew was compliance and enforcement. And, related to that, the plant had two other key safety issues: They needed employee involvement in all 9 Key Elements of Safety, not only in training, and they needed to know how to coach employees on the floor.

Guess where I started at Plant B? You guessed it…I spent a lot of time with Al on the floor. I needed him to understand the coaching and put it into practice. His habit of writing up employees for every little thing was creating two problems: First, his approach was doing very little to engage employees to change the culture. And second, writing up employees was an effective deterrent only when he was around, since the supervisors certainly weren't writing up anyone.

Al was excellent at implementing the compliance, policies, and procedures sections of the 9 Key Elements of Safety but less effective in influencing the leadership team and getting hourly employees involved. He was of the mindset that employees should just follow the rules and ask no questions.

And if they failed to follow the rules, he wrote them up.

As part of my coaching, I worked one-on-one with Al on the floor. When I saw someone working safely, I recommended he have a two-way positive reinforcement conversation. But Al screwed it up completely. Instead of giving the employee specific recognition, he said, "Good job working safely."

We tried it again and again, but Al just could not get words of specific recognition to flow out of his mouth. So I took him into a nearby office and role-played the technique with him, but still he struggled. I was determined to help him change his approach. Al was the safety leader, so it was important that he model this technique; otherwise, he would struggle to get other leaders to teach it. I visited Plant B once a month for three months until Al got this technique down. Once he was comfortable with the technique, I asked him to set up meetings with the leadership team to conduct this same type of training.

After we implemented these coaching techniques at Plant B, the plant's safety results improved dramatically over the next six months (the second half of FY 2003). When I began this coaching in the middle of FY 2003, the plant had an OIR of 6.5, but they achieved an OIR of 5.1 in FY 2004, 4.5 in FY 2005, and 2.3 in FY 2006. In just three years, they were well on their way to world-class safety results, and Al was mastering and teaching the techniques!

I repeated this training for the leadership teams at the other three plants. Two of them achieved world-class status in just three years. At one, the OIR results went from 4.2 in FY 2004 to 2.7 in FY 2005 and to 1.7 in FY 2006; the other plant achieved OIRs of 3.2 in FY 2004, 2.1 in FY 2005, and 1.7 in FY 2006.

Another plant that made phenomenal gains during this period was the Central California plant where I'd started my career with Company #2. When I arrived in 1999, this plant had ranked last, #50, with an OIR of 21.0, and, by 2004, it achieved an OIR of 2.2. In both 2005 and 2006, the plant achieved world-class status, with OIRs of 1.8 and 1.5, respectively, and won Safety Plant of the Year both years. Between 1999 and 2005, that plant rose from last place to one of the top five plants in the organization.

Plant C

Located about thirty miles east of the plant where I'd started with Company #2, Plant C had 400 employees year-round and 1,000 employees during tomato season. The plant management team was known for producing a superior tomato product regarded as the best in the fresh whole, peeled and diced tomato business.

Plant C was where I had day-to-day responsibility, which meant that all the training I did with the other four plants took place either before or after tomato season.

Like all the plants at Company #2, Plant C had a pretty good safety process in place, yet they had a tough time engaging the hourly associates. The safety process was primarily run by management. At the time, Plant C's OIR was 7.1.

Knowing all this about Plant C, I decided to start the training a little differently. I first met with the plant management team on the production floor to observe employees. The production manager, John, was the person I had to sell the safety process to, which was no small task. John was aggressive and production-oriented, and not at all receptive to the need for a safety process.

While the rest of the management team stood back about fifty feet, John and I observed an hourly employee as he worked.

"What do you see this employee doing that is safe?" I asked John.

"Well, he's locking out the equipment," he replied.

"I'm going to try an approach and I just want you to observe," I said to John.

I launched into my positive reinforcement approach with the employee. "John and I noticed that you locked out this piece of equipment, and we just wanted to say thank you for doing that. How can we get others at this plant to lock out just like you did?"

The employee's face lit up, and I could see John was surprised by his reaction. I later asked John what had surprised him. "I didn't think that thanking someone would produce that type of reaction," he said.

Then I discussed with John that employees don't hear good things from management often enough. We dictate the culture. We tell employees what to run, how to run it, and when to run it, but when it comes to safety, we say nothing.

"John, would you be interested in knowing how to dictate safety at this plant like you do production?" I knew if I won John over, everyone else would fall in line.

"Yes," he answered immediately, and he said it with such enthusiasm that I knew he was committed.

I was successful in winning his support that day, and it was the beginning of a great professional and personal relationship.

John then set up meetings so I could talk to the plant leadership, and guess what I talked about? The two-way technique, of course. With John leading the way as safety champion, Plant C jumped onboard in a hurry. Employees were writing job safety analyses, participating on safety audits, leading safety meetings, and actively participating in the safety committees. Most importantly, employees were conducting "be safe" observations, and supervisors were recognizing employees for safe behaviors and coaching employees on the risk of their unsafe behaviors. This was exactly the type of engagement Plant C was looking for. As a result, its safety numbers rapidly improved, and continued to improve over the next three years as activities such as these became a part of the culture at the plant.

In the span of just one year, from FY 2003 to FY 2004, Plant C's OIR results fell dramatically from 7.1 to 3.2. In FY 2005, the OIR was reduced again, to 2.1, and by the end of FY 2006, Plant C achieved world-class status with an OIR of 1.7.

By the end of FY 2006, the results were so good at all five of my plants that Brian, formerly at the Pittsburgh plant and now the global director of EHS, and Gary, the new North America director for EHS, asked me to join the corporate EHS team. This was the third time Brian had asked, and I knew it might be my final opportunity to join the corporate team.

Lessons Learned

○ Standardizing the coaching approach and the process keeps things simple and consistent. Supervisors at all five of my plants coached employees using the two-way conversation.

○ Positive reinforcement makes employees feel good about what they are doing. In all five plants, the general feedback was that employees were happy to receive positive reinforcement for working safely. It was the beginning of getting employees to think for themselves and take responsibility for their own safety.

○ Even coaching moments can be positive. The two-way conversation is non-confrontational, although it does challenge employees to think about the risks and what could happen to them.

○ It was evident that our safety professionals knew how to implement compliance processes, policies, and procedures, but they struggled with the culture side of safety. In all five plants, the management teams believed the coaching techniques I introduced were game changers in helping their employees focus on creating a safety culture.

○ As a safety professional, when you can illustrate to plant leadership how you will bring value to the team, the operations team will get onboard. Safety professionals often overlook how important this is. I saw this happen at all five plants, especially at Plant C where I spent time on the operations floor with the production manager, John.

chapter six

The Safety Challenge: What Are Your Employees Doing Right Now?

With my promotion to the corporate EHS team at Company #2, I became the senior manager of safety for the western region. Along with the promotion, I gained nine new plants. I was now responsible for twelve plants in the U.S. and two plants in Canada. What I didn't know at the time was that I would also have the opportunity to begin standardizing the leadership coaching methods throughout the organization and, down the line, help in shaping the company's safety culture.

By this time, I'd worked as a safety professional for seventeen years, and I'd invested countless hours in investigating injuries, interviewing employees, and analyzing data. One key fact had remained consistent throughout my safety career, and as I continued teaching and coaching, I found myself coming back to it. There are only two reasons why injuries happen in manufacturing: unsafe acts (90 percent of the time) or unsafe conditions (10 percent of the time). Most organizations spend 90 percent of their time fixing conditions, yet 90 percent of injuries result from unsafe acts that workers commit.

In my previous role, I'd used a tried-and-true process that had successfully reduced unsafe acts: identifying the top three sources of loss, correcting unsafe acts through two-way conversations, and using positive reinforcement with employees who were working safely. Through that process, my focus was to encourage the plant leadership teams to get involved in coaching employees on the floor and in teaching their supervisors to coach employees.

But in my new role, I'd gained additional responsibility for nine new plants, and I didn't have the capacity to do a thorough assessment of the safety culture of each new plant. I had to find a way to quickly assess the culture. So when I went into each plant for the first time, I started asking, "How safely do our employees work when management is not around?"

This question soon led me to come up with a safety challenge for supervisors. The challenge was this: If I did not observe any unsafe acts by a supervisor's employees in a defined fifteen-minute period, the supervisor would win $20. The goals of the challenge were to see how much confidence the supervisor had in his or her team, and to see how much work I needed to do with the supervisor on coaching.

The criteria for the safety challenge were as follows:

- ○ Supervisors had to supervise a minimum of ten employees to participate. The thinking was that anybody can observe one or two employees all day, but when you have ten employees spread out, it's tough to keep an eye on all of them at the same time.

- ○ Supervisors were not to tell employees we were doing the challenge. This was to ensure a fair challenge, without prior notification. I typically noticed evaporative unsafe acts, meaning that employees corrected their own unsafe acts when the boss walked into the area. For example, employees would put in earplugs, flip down safety glasses, and follow safety procedures correctly.

- ○ All employees of the supervisor (a minimum of ten) had to work safely for fifteen minutes.

- ○ The site safety manager would be the referee and timekeeper. For example, if I saw an unsafe act during the fifteen-minute plant tour and the supervisor missed it, the site safety manager would be there to settle any disagreements.

- ○ I would put up $20 for the challenge and the supervisor was required to put up $10, just to make sure the supervisor had some skin in the game. The site safety manager would hold the money and would also win the money, at least temporarily, if the supervisor lost the challenge (meaning that at least one employee was observed committing an unsafe act).

○ If the supervisor lost the challenge, the supervisor could earn back the $10 by practicing and demonstrating the classroom technique with the employee who had committed the unsafe act.

○ If the supervisor won the challenge (meaning that none of the supervisor's employees was observed committing an unsafe act), the vice president of operations would send the supervisor a congratulatory email to share with the winning team.

The first time we did this challenge was in late 2006 at a plant in Southern California with a group of about twelve supervisors and their production manager. I slapped $20 down in front of each supervisor and described the rules of the challenge. All supervisors were quiet, and several minutes passed without anyone taking me up on the challenge.

With every passing minute, I could see the production manager was getting more livid. He stared at his #1 go-getter, a young floor supervisor. "Take the guy up on the challenge!" he barked.

She hesitated and stumbled over her words as she tried to back out. Finally she spoke up. "I don't have $10 to challenge him."

The production manager pulled out a $10 bill and slapped it on the table. "I'll pay your ten bucks."

The tension hung in the air. I had not anticipated this turn of events. The challenge was designed to be voluntary, without any pressure. In fact, it was supposed to be fun.

After a few tense moments, I finally stepped in to defuse the situation. "Let's not force anyone to do this," I said to the production manager.

"No, it's okay," the supervisor said. "I want to take the challenge."

The other eleven supervisors wanted nothing to do with this challenge, so I asked them and the production manager to leave.

That left the safety manager, the supervisor, and me in the room. I started going over the rules once again. But before I could finish, the safety manager and I were suddenly called to an emergency meeting, so we agreed to resume the challenge in two hours.

Two hours later, we met in production area #1. As we entered the area, I noticed that all twenty-five employees were watching me carefully. Something didn't feel right. I suspected they knew what was coming.

Within a few minutes, a line jammed up with product, but the machine operator didn't even move. Instead, the supervisor who was taking the challenge walked over to the line and safely unjammed the product.

"You cheated!" I hollered out to her.

"No, I did not," she replied calmly. "I did not cheat."

We continued debating, and I kept insisting that what I'd witnessed was not normal behavior. "There's no way in the world that the operator would not *immediately* make a move to unjam the product," I said. "Unless, of course, you told the operator there's a bet on the table."

The supervisor continued to deny that she'd said anything to her employees. I was still suspicious, but after using up five of our precious fifteen minutes debating, I decided to drop it and went back to looking for unsafe acts.

After a few more minutes had passed without any unsafe acts, I started getting nervous. I hate to lose.

"Listen, I'll make you a deal," I said to the supervisor. "I'll give you your $10 right now if you call off the bet."

"No way," the supervisor replied, apparently feeling quite confident.

About eleven minutes into the bet, I was sweating and very anxious, thinking I was about to lose the challenge. But a minute later, an employee came down the stairs not holding onto the handrail.

"I win!" I yelled.

Just to be clear, I was not celebrating that the employee was working unsafely. I'm naturally very competitive and, in a situation like this, I tend to temporarily get caught up in the heat of competition, and my strong desire to win takes over. But this was one bet I would have been happy to lose.

This was how the very first safety challenge kicked off at Company #2, and it was later incorporated into all coaching sessions for supervisors. I learned a useful lesson from this first challenge and immediately added a new rule requiring that the challenge begin immediately following the classroom training.

For the next two years, I conducted the safety challenge at every plant I visited in the western region. Plant managers along the East Coast soon heard about the work I was doing with the plant management team, along with the safety challenge, so Dan, the VP of operations, asked me to conduct this training at the twenty plants in the eastern region. Out of a total of thirty-four plants that I visited between 2006 and 2008, only five plants won the challenge.

While these challenges were going on in full force, I was given the opportunity to provide input on the design for Company #2's brand-new, "accident-free" manufacturing plant in South Carolina. This new facility was going to be a state-of-the-art, ergonomically designed plant where employees did not have to manually dump products, as they did at most of our plants. The machines were well guarded. Powered Industrial Truck (PIT) areas were well designed with dock locks and signals and blind-spot mirrors. The walking and working surfaces were slip-resistant, fall protection areas had anchor points, platforms had safety gates, not chains, and robots palletized products once everything was packaged.

To reduce the risks to hands and fingers when products jammed up, production equipment came with CAT3 protection, a double safety protection to prevent machinery from starting up unexpectedly. The goal for this plant—and all plants—was to make sure all employees went home the same way they came in.

From an engineering standpoint, this plant was designed to be accident-free; it featured the latest innovations available at the time, and the built-in safety measures were so comprehensive that I figured I'd never win a safety challenge here.

There were no injuries in the first two months of production at this new facility, which was to be expected. However, in month three we had three injuries, and in month five there were another two. The bad news kept on coming, and by the end of the plant's first year in operation, we'd had a total of thirteen recordable injuries.

We could not believe what was happening at this state-of-the-art plant. It was designed to be accident-free, yet in its first year, its OIR was 5.8. The corporate OIR was 1.0.

In our injury analyses, we noted that only one injury resulted from an unsafe condition, a piece of equipment dripping oil. An employee had slipped in that oil and hurt his back while trying to brace himself.

The other twelve injuries resulted from unsafe acts: three employees tumbled down the stairs because they didn't hold onto the handrails, three employees received lacerations from handling packaging materials without cut-resistant gloves, one employee got dust in his eyes from not wearing safety glasses while driving his forklift in the warehouse, three employees had back injuries from lifting and restacking rework product, and two employees tripped over product on the floor because they failed to clean up after themselves. Basically we had twelve recordable injuries in a new facility that was designed to be free of hazards, simply because employees did not follow safety rules and, therefore, created their own hazards. We had sixty-year-old plants that had better safety records than this one.

These results confirmed my belief that you can't completely engineer out all risks of injury. Whenever there are people in a plant, there are safety risks; *the only plant that is truly risk-free is one that has closed for business.* No matter how safe the plant conditions are, employees must take responsibility to work safely. That's more likely to happen if a strong safety culture has been created in the company by recognizing employees for working safely.

In my role as the fixer, I was sent to the South Carolina plant to help get their safety process under control. For five months, I worked with the leadership team on the employee coaching approaches, and finally we started to see things trend in a positive direction. The plant's OIR improved from 5.8 to 3.1 within those first five months, and the following year it continued to decrease to a 2.2.

On a side note, I was wrong in assuming I'd never be able to win a safety challenge at the "accident-free" plant in South Carolina. I conducted the challenge at this plant in early 2010 and won when a forklift driver failed to turn around as he backed up the forklift.

Lessons Learned

○ Safety 101: Injuries happen in two ways: through unsafe acts or unsafe conditions. Most safety professionals spend their time correcting unsafe conditions because these conditions don't talk back to leaders. But spending your time fixing conditions yields at best a 9 percent return (10 percent unsafe conditions × 90 percent activities), not a good return on the time invested. Spending time correcting unsafe acts, however, yields a return of 81 percent (90 percent unsafe acts × 90 percent activities). Unsafe acts can be corrected if supervisors are properly taught how to coach employees on the operations floor.

○ The safety challenge was designed to answer this question: How safely do our employees work when management is not around? One reason that most supervisors didn't take me up on the challenge was because they didn't know the answer to that question; they didn't know what their employees would be doing as we walked into their production areas.

○ No matter how safe the plant is by design, unsafe behaviors can still take place if a safety culture has not been created. Even though the new plant had been designed without hazards, employees fell down stairs because they did not hold onto handrails, hurt their backs by incorrectly lifting reworked products, and were hurt by tripping over clutter they'd forgotten to clean up. When employees skipped safety procedures, even the safest conditions possible could not protect them from injury.

chapter seven

An Engaged Employee is a Safe Employee

In 2010, I was given the opportunity to take another big company to world-class safety performance, and so I left Company #2 to begin the next chapter of my life. I had mixed feelings about leaving, however. After all, Company #2 had taught me one of the greatest safety systems I'd seen. But I knew I was ready to use the experience I'd gained to help another company achieve the same success.

Company #3 was a large food company headquartered in Nebraska. I became the director of safety for the specialty and frozen foods business unit and was responsible for twelve plants in the U.S.

Company #3 was a matrix organization, a different organizational structure than I was used to. In this type of organization you have a direct boss, but you also indirectly report to one or two others in the organization. My direct boss was Tom, the senior director of safety, and I also indirectly reported to Tim, the VP of operations. The good news is that Tom and Tim were both aligned with the work they expected me to do. I had met Tom and his boss, Jim, the VP of environmental health and safety (EHS), three years earlier at a gathering of food industry EHS professionals, and they became my mentors at Company #3.

Tom, Tim, and Jim all sat on the twenty-member supply chain senior leadership team. On my first day at the new company, several members of the team started asking me about Company #2's safety processes and the differences between the two companies. Everyone seemed to know about Company #2, its strong safety culture, and its world-class safety status, so I wasn't surprised that my new colleagues wanted some insights into Company #2. I was in no position to start making comparisons yet, however, so for the first few weeks I focused on my new job and observed and learned everything I could about my new employer.

One statistic I learned right away was that Company #3's overall OIR was 3.6, better than the industry average of 4.5, but a long way from Company #2's world-class OIR, which was 0.98 when I left. My business unit was near the corporate average.

Just one month into my new role, I went out to dinner with the supply chain leadership team. Clearly the team members had been waiting for this opportunity. From the moment I arrived, I was bombarded with questions about my former employer.

"What was the OIR at Company #2?"

"What engagement activities were employees involved with?"

"Did Company #2 do perception surveys?"

The questions came at me so fast that I had to abandon my dinner. Jim, my boss's boss, finally broke into the conversation and came to my rescue.

"Hey, how 'bout we let the guy eat his dinner, please," he said. "Keith can't answer any questions with his mouth full of food."

The conversation immediately came to a halt and I was able to resume eating. But after less than thirty seconds of silence, Jim spoke up once again. "So, Keith, now that it's finally quiet, I can ask you my top three questions." Everyone laughed. "First, what audit systems did the company use? Second, did the employees lead the safety meetings? And finally, how soon can we expect to see results?" Once again I set down my knife and fork to answer his questions.

After I finished eating, with great fanfare I tapped my spoon on my drinking glass as if I were at a wedding. "If I could have your attention for a moment, I have an announcement."

When the talking died down, I continued. "For several weeks now, all of you and many plant managers have been asking about my former employer, and tonight I'm glad I had the opportunity to answer many of your follow-up questions. Some of you have also been asking me to assess this company's strengths and opportunities, but up until now I didn't feel I could properly respond. You'll be happy to know that I finally have some answers for you."

All conversation ceased and every eye was on me as I began.

"First off, I want to let you know that I've been very impressed by this company and its many strengths, starting with its awesome leadership. In addition to that, there are three specific areas where I think you're particularly strong: One, you're doing a great job in compliance with policies and procedures. Two, you're being very diligent in recording and tracking injuries. And three, your safety audit system is second to none."

I paused for a moment to let my news sink in. Several people around the table were nodding their heads, and they seemed pleased with my assessment.

"But that doesn't mean there isn't some room for improvement," I continued. "I've seen two key areas where I believe we can add to what we're already doing. The first is in analyzing injury losses and the second is in coaching supervisors."

I went on to tell the leadership team why these two issues were at the top of my list. I explained that analyzing injury loss is important because it's at the heart of accident prevention, which I saw as the main gap at Company #3. There was no process in place to investigate the top three injury losses, put proactive activities in place to reduce those losses, or measure progress against those activities.

The second issue, coaching supervisors, was more specifically about the need to engage supervisors in the safety process. I told the team that the company was already doing a great job involving hourly associates in its continuous improvement efforts, but the supervisors had been left out of the process.

I'd learned from experience that if the supervisors aren't engaged in the process, the employees won't be engaged, either. If the company wanted to see real improvements in safety, supervisors needed to be included.

Following my comments, there were a few more questions and then we were able to finish dinner, finally.

I left that meeting feeling that Company #3 expected a lot from me, and there was no time to lose. My role was to make sure plants worked on things that drove results. While Company #2 had had a well-developed safety culture, Company #3 was still rooted in compliance, and I knew the results they wanted could be accomplished only by changing the culture. One sure way to start achieving those results was to get the supervisors more engaged in the safety process. I needed to start coaching as soon as I could arrange it.

The following week I held my first coaching session for supervisors at a Michigan plant, using the very same coaching techniques I'd taught at Company #2 eleven years before. The content was more focused, however, and covered not only this plant's top three injury loss sources—slips and falls, manual material handling, and struck by/against injuries— but also the behaviors related to those top three injury losses. It was a real advantage to be able to address both topics at the same time.

The session was structured very much like the sessions I'd conducted at Company #2: I first role-played the coaching techniques with the supervisors in a classroom setting, then I took them out to the production floor to practice the techniques.

For employees who were working safely, the supervisors were instructed to use the positive reinforcement technique that I'd taught to Company #2. These interactions would go as follows:

"I appreciate that you…(held onto the handrails, cleaned up the cluttered area, lifted safely by using your legs and not your back, locked out the equipment, etc.). How can I get others to do it just like you?"

The supervisor was instructed to stay quiet at this point and wait for the employee's response, then again thank the employee for his or her specific safe work behavior. Over the years, I'd seen time and time again that positive reinforcement is a powerful motivator in encouraging employees to work safely when supervisors are not present.

When supervisors observed employees working unsafely, the supervisors were to use the two-way coaching technique, which was designed to identify unsafe behavior and ensure it did not happen again:

"I noticed that you…(did not hold onto the handrails, did not clean up the cluttered area, did not use your legs while lifting, did not lock out the equipment, etc.). What is the worst that can happen if you continue to work unsafely?"

The supervisor was instructed to stay quiet at this point and wait for the employee's response, then ask the employee, "Why would you take that chance/take that risk?"

Earlier in this Michigan session, I'd offered all the participants the opportunity to take my safety challenge, another initiative I'd created while I was at Company #2. The challenge typically happens within the first ten minutes of the supervisor training, following the classroom training, and just before the participants go out to the production floor to practice the coaching techniques.

Only a few participants in the Michigan session had chosen to take part in the safety challenge, which was typical. The low rate of participation didn't surprise me; it simply confirmed that supervisors knew that unsafe acts were happening on their shifts and they didn't want to lose their $10.

After I'd finished presenting the two-way conversation approach to this group, I decided I'd revisit the safety challenge we'd done at the beginning of the session and try to get some specific feedback.

"Supervisors, why did you not take me up on the safety challenge?"

They obviously hadn't expected my blunt question, but their responses were revealing in their honesty:

- My Oscar will lose the money for me by doing something unsafe.

- I have not corrected every unsafe act in the past and now it's the norm for some team members to work unsafely.

- Because the safety challenge takes place immediately after the training session, I figured when we walked into the work area we'd probably see more evaporative unsafe acts (unsafe acts that temporarily disappear because someone is watching) and employees would put in earplugs, flip-down safety glasses, and put on hard hats.

○ I have not thanked employees in the past for working safely, so they will be more likely to work unsafely.

After hearing those answers, I asked, "If you know your employees are working unsafely, why don't you get proactive? You need to have discussions with them before someone works unsafely and ends up getting injured. You already know who will do something unsafely and you know what that unsafe act will be. This would be a great opportunity to conduct one-on-one coaching with those employees before they have another chance to work unsafely."

I also told them that they should talk about and reinforce their expectations every day, and suggested that during shift huddles they could discuss both safe and unsafe behaviors they'd observed the previous day.

After many years of conducting this safety training, I know that supervisors don't typically talk to employees about working safely, and that's precisely the reason I coach them. They don't feel comfortable coaching employees—and neither did I when I was a supervisor. This gap is typical in most organizations. Many leaders tell us what to do, but very few teach us how to do it. My training sessions teach how to coach employees in a caring manner that will influence their behavior if they practice the techniques for thirty days.

I'm always tickled to see what happens when supervisors follow my suggestion and actually learn the techniques and practice them consistently for thirty days. Whenever I go back to the plants for a follow-up visit, virtually every supervisor who lost the safety challenge the first time around asks to go back to their work areas so they can win the bet during that second visit. I don't necessarily follow through and repeat the challenge, but I love the enthusiasm.

The fact that those supervisors even make that request tells me two things: Their confidence is high because they have been practicing for at least thirty days straight, and they have started positively reinforcing the safe behaviors they've seen in their teams, especially in their Oscars.

After the introduction of supervisor coaching at Company #3, the specialty/frozen foods division beat their annual OIR targets for two years straight, achieving an OIR of 2.4 in FY 2012 and a world-class OIR of 1.7 in FY 2013. This was a huge accomplishment, particularly because this division had previously missed their target OIRs for four consecutive years.

That exceptional performance level was the result of key activities that had helped develop the safety culture:

   ○ Identifying the top three loss sources;

   ○ Reducing risks by implementing best practices;

   ○ Developing the plant leadership, including the plant safety manager, by teaching them to coach employees on the plant floor.

By consistently applying these proven coaching techniques, the teams were successful in driving the safety culture in this business unit at Company #3.

After achieving consistently high performance levels, I was promoted to senior director of safety in 2013 and started working with 110 plants, 20 of which process French fries for a fast-food chain.

Lessons Learned

○ Supervisors typically know which unsafe acts will be committed, and by whom, in their respective areas. I challenged supervisors to talk one-on-one with those employees about the risks associated with unsafe acts or to discuss in the daily shift huddle any unsafe acts they observed the previous day. I encouraged them to communicate their safety expectations to employees every day, whether in groups or in informal one-on-one sessions.

○ Positively reinforcing safe behavior helps employees feel good about their own behavior and motivates them to continue working safely when supervisors are not present. Positive reinforcement is usually what sets world-class safety organizations apart and puts them in the Independent Stage of safety.

○ I always encourage supervisors to practice these coaching techniques for thirty consecutive days, because that is said to be the length of time needed for a new activity to become a habit. I can tell by their enthusiasm that they've been practicing, and that enthusiasm is likely to help their employees also feel good about working safely. I tell supervisors that the difference between me coaching employees and the average supervisor coaching employees is called "practice."

chapter eight

Get Uncomfortable

After reducing the OIR of the specialty/frozen foods unit from 3.6 to 1.7—a decrease of 53 percent—in just two years, my boss and I agreed that I should help out the business unit that makes French fries for some of the largest fast-food chains around the world.

This business unit, which included twenty plants, had an OIR of 3.91 for FYs 2011 and 2012. At Company #3, an OIR that high was considered "red performance," indicating that the business unit had not met its goals.

This business unit could not seem to get over the hump in the area of safety, although many aspects of safety were well under control: They had mastered basic compliance with governmental regulations, policies, and procedures, and they had a proactive safety system that included comprehensive annual safety plans created by management to prevent injuries.

This business unit's major challenge was to get employees to take ownership of their own safety and then engage in the safety process by, for example, leading safety meetings, writing job safety analyses and participating in safety audits.

The operations leadership team of this business unit was looking for something that would take this group to the next level of safety. They had done what was "comfortable" and, as a result, they weren't happy with their safety performance because too many employees were still getting injured. The other business units were "green" but this one was "red" since this unit was experiencing twice as many injuries, on average, than the other business units. The enterprise was trying to get to an OIR of 2.0 or less and, to do that, this unit had to perform better. They needed to at least come down to a 2.7 to reach a milestone we'd set for the company.

I sat down with my boss, Tom, the VP of Environment, Health, Safety, and Security, and discussed the need to improve their safety performance. We agreed that I should go and provide assistance.

Tom wanted to make the initial contact and clear it with the business unit first. He told me he had called the two safety directors, Tony and Ward, and presented it to them like this: "I want Keith Bardney to come out and work with you two on taking your safety process to the next level."

"Yeah?" said Tony. "So what does that mean? What's he going to do?"

"Keith is going to help you create a safety culture that will bring remarkable results," Tom explained. "You won't believe the difference his approach will make."

"Well, we've had a few people from corporate safety cycle through here already," said Ward. "They were all determined to fix this safety challenge, but no one's ever made any lasting change. Why do you think this guy will be any different?"

"And how long will it take to create a safety culture?" said Tony.

"Just trust me," Tom said.

He understood why Tony and Ward were less than enthusiastic about having me come out to help, but he'd given them no choice.

I also understood why they were resistant. When the corporate office sends its people to fix a problem, the plant staff members often refer to this as the Seagull Approach: The corporate representative flies in, drops crap all over the place by telling you what you need to do without showing you how to do it, leaves a long to-do list, then flies off.

So I called Tony and Ward to explain my approach. They told me that the operations team was looking for something that would make a lasting difference, but Tom hadn't told them enough about my approach, and they doubted it would change anything.

I told Tony and Ward I'd show management how to coach employees on the floor through positive reinforcement and two-way conversation techniques. I also mentioned that the training would reinforce the behaviors that management wanted to see, and coaching would discourage those behaviors they didn't. This would not only change the game but also get employees to look out for each other, which is the key to sustainability that eventually leads to world-class safety.

Tony and Ward liked what I was saying, but they wanted to see the coaching in action. We decided to start with one of their biggest plants, located in Washington state, where Marty was the plant manager. I scheduled the usual three-shift supervisor safety training, and Marty, Tony, and Ward attended all three sessions.

Marty had been around for over thirty years and was well respected in the organization. In fact, he held so much sway that my first presentation would make or break me, depending on the feedback that Marty gave to the organization. The agenda was as follows:

- ○ My background

- ○ Safety expectations and challenge

- ○ Coaching techniques

- ○ Role-playing

- ○ Validation of understanding through role-playing

- ○ Questions and homework assigned; this involved conducting a minimum of one touchpoint daily for thirty days

- ○ 1:1 Job shadowing of supervisors

Marty sat in on the first presentation and was totally engaged in it. He went out on the floor and practiced the coaching techniques, encouraged supervisors to try it, and reinforced to all participants the need to practice these techniques daily for thirty days.

Marty really seemed to like my main point in this presentation, which was, "You don't have to spend any money to make safety happen at your plant." Another key theme that I talk about is, "Safety made simple." I used these terms because safety is just one of the many balls that operations people need to juggle. In these coaching sessions, I made my point by comparing safety with baseball, starting with my own baseball career:

"I was a catcher for two years in high school, and I treat employee behaviors the way that the umpire calls balls and strikes. You all know how this goes… The pitch comes zinging in and immediately the umpire calls it. "Ball one!" When the next pitch comes in like a rocket, the umpire calls, "Ball two!" Then on the third pitch, the umpire doesn't hesitate for even a split second before he calls out, "Strike one!"

Never have I heard an umpire say, "Ball! Uh, no, I mean strike! Hmm, you know, I'm just not sure what the call is!" With the umpire, there's no gray area—to him it's either a ball or a strike. And it's the same with employee behavior. An employee is either working safely or unsafely. There's no gray area here, either.

At this point, I prompted the participants to complete the following:

If the employee is working safe, you should say…

If the employee is working unsafe, you should say…

Figure 3.

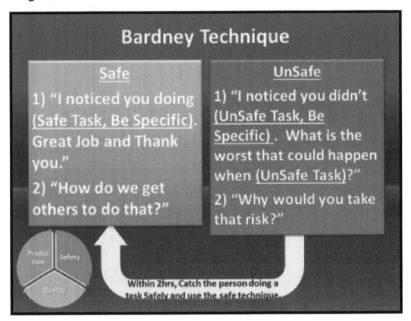

Marty liked the simplicity of the training so much that he participated in coaching supervisors on the floor. His glowing feedback on the training earned me the right to hold training sessions at the other nineteen plants in this business unit.

Tony and Ward also sat in on the first session to monitor participants' feedback, and they liked the training so much that they decided to come on the road with me to visit the other nineteen plants. Tony, Ward, and I became road warriors as we worked all three shifts at 95 percent of the business unit facilities.

The more employees we trained, the more that the culture of Company #3 shifted toward the Independent/Interdependent organization that Tony talked about all the time. (See Figure 4.)

Figure 4.

INTERDEPENDENT STAGE
Employees look out for each other

The majority of the staff is convinced that health and safety are important, from both a moral and an economic viewpoint.

Management recognizes that many factors lead to accidents, and the root causes likely stem from management decisions.

Frontline staff members accept responsibility for their own and others' health and safety.

Management recognizes the importance of all employees feeling valued and being treated fairly.

The plant puts significant effort into proactive measures to prevent accidents.

Safety performance is actively monitored using all data available.

A healthy lifestyle is promoted and non-work accidents are also monitored.

The prevention of all injuries or harm to employees is an accepted core value.

The plant has not experienced a recordable accident or high-potential incident in years, but there is no feeling of complacency.

The plant uses a range of leading and lagging indicators to monitor performance, but the plant is not performance-driven; it has confidence in its safety processes.

> The plant strives to be better and find better hazard-control approaches.
>
> All employees share the belief that health and safety are critical aspects of their jobs and accept that preventing non-work injuries is important.
>
> The plant invests considerable effort in promoting health and safety at home.

Tony, Ward, and I visited all twenty plants within six months and conducted the same coaching training at each one. The responses from participants were very favorable, and since fewer people were experiencing injuries, the organization's OIR dropped quickly; within just one year, the OIR in this business unit dropped 20 percent, from 3.13 in FY 2013 to 2.60 in FY 2014. (See Figure 5.) Both Tony and Ward said that the coaching training was exactly what they had been missing.

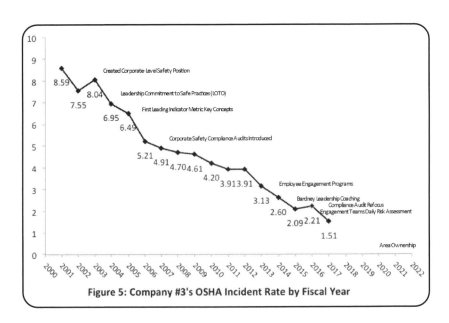

Figure 5: Company #3's OSHA Incident Rate by Fiscal Year

At the end of FY 2014, Ward returned to a plant in Washington for family reasons, so I ended up working with Tony one-on-one. Tony was a quiet and very effective leader. He had a great vision of what this business unit needed in order to get to world-class safety performance.

Tony was uncomfortable being comfortable. He wanted even more employee engagement because he knew that was the route to sustainable world-class safety. So, in addition to the leadership coaching on the floor, Tony and I discussed conducting risk predictions in FY 2015, particularly those that employees face every day at work.

Each day, the management team and hourly associates identified areas of risk for that day and implemented countermeasures to reduce the chance of an injury. In addition, employees identified individual risks and managed against them. Here are some examples:

○ Using the correct procedures when unjamming product to ensure their safety.

○ Beeping the horn when entering high-traffic areas with forklifts and slowing down to prevent hitting pedestrians.

○ Identifying all new or temporary employees working in the area and showing them safety procedures to reduce their risk of injury.

○ Wearing proper PPE when cleaning with sodium hydroxide (caustic soda).

The risks were rated on a scale of 1 (low) to 5 (high); for any risk above a 3.5, countermeasures were required to be in place.

The risk-prediction process was important because it was another way to get hourly associates directly engaged in the safety process. Risk prediction and coaching employees on the operations floor changed the game for this organization. At the end of FY 2015, the OIR was reduced again, to 2.14, but rose slightly, to 2.21, in FY 2016. In FY 2017, the OIR decreased significantly, to 1.51. After experiencing three straight years of red performance, this business unit finally achieved world-class safety status.

This business unit separated from Company #3 in November 2016 and I truly miss them. The thing I liked most about this organization is that they never, ever gave up on safety. They were never satisfied with their safety performance and they were comfortable being uncomfortable. Continuous improvement is in their blood.

My hat is off to Tony, Ward, Rick, Wayne, Fred, Rick, and the rest of the operations team. They trusted me and gave me an opportunity to make a difference in the lives of our employees, and I will always be grateful for that. They are simply the best.

Lessons Learned

○ Coaching behaviors are not an exact science, which is why it was hard for Tom to explain them. Coaching uses soft skills, but the average operations person does not utilize those skills as option one; in fact, these skills are more likely the last option on the list. This business unit did not get excited by simply hearing about coaching employees, but when they were able to see the coaching in action, they quickly changed their attitudes.

○ In baseball, the pitch is either a ball or strike; in safety, employees either work safely or they do not. It's that straightforward. And the responses to these behaviors are also straightforward: If employees work safely, leaders should positively reinforce that behavior with verbal recognition. If employees work unsafely, leaders should coach employees in a caring manner.

○ For this business unit, employee coaching and risk prediction were the two missing pieces of the safety puzzle. Through coaching, the team made huge improvements in its safety process over a three-year period. And by introducing risk prediction for every activity, the business unit was able to achieve world-class safety. These two activities also got employees even more engaged in the safety process to the point that they started feeling ownership. This is one key indication that the organization had reached the Interdependent Stage in its safety process.

Conclusion

My safety journey has been about creating a zero-injury culture by engaging employees in the safety process and keeping them out of the hospital. I have been taught and trained by many great leaders, who have helped me accomplish this objective.

My hope is that you were able to relate to some of these stories and can use my experience to help you along in your own journey. I understand the obstacles and struggles you will face, and I say to you: It is worth it. It is worth seeing employees go home exactly the way they came into the workplace.

The process is simple and these results are achievable if you're willing to commit to the process and build it one step at a time. Whether you're an introvert or an extrovert, experienced or inexperienced, compliance-driven or culture-driven, you can do this—and do it well—if you want to make a difference and you're not afraid of a little bit of work. We all have a unique style and a unique way of doing things; so find what works with your style and fine-tune it until it's effective.

Safety is not about theories and concepts. It is not about textbook learning, and it's much more than writing policies and merely complying with OSHA regulations. I've learned that the most effective approach to safety is actually much more straightforward than that.

Simply put, safety is about people and how we interact with them on a daily basis to reduce their risk at work and home. How well you do that will make or break your safety process.

About the Author

Keith Bardney is a passionate, energetic, and respected safety professional. Since 1989, he has worked with multi-billion-dollar food manufacturing companies to keep their employees injury-free. He is currently the Lead Coach for KYB Consulting & Coaching and previously held safety positions for multi-billion dollar food manufacturing companies. His career also has included positions in quality control, research and development, production supervision, and human resource management.

Keith holds a bachelor's degree in occupational safety from Illinois State University and a master's degree in occupational safety and health/environmental management from Columbia Southern University. He has a Certified Safety Professional (CSP) designation and is an active member of the American Society of Safety Engineers.

Early in his career, Keith learned that safety is a people business. He leads by example, develops leaders, and engages employees in a caring manner. *Creating a Zero-Incident Culture* is the story of how he created a sustainable safety culture in which incidents are seen as preventable. Keith knows firsthand that the outcome is worth the effort.

Acknowledgments

I owe a huge thank you to my editor, Brenda Quinn, who truly is a word whiz. Her attention to detail and her knowledge of how to present information to readers were invaluable.

So many people have provided inspiration and encouragement along the way, especially my first safety teacher and loving mom, Pearl Bardney, who has since passed, and my two children, who taught me patience. I'm also indebted to Tony Campbell, Ward Miller, and Chris Bingham for encouraging me to write this book, and to my many mentors, not only for coaching me but also for being great examples of what they taught: Charles Angell, Terry Spencer, John Wayhart, Allen Ferrini, Wayne Koch, Brian Shuttleworth, Gary Thomas, Dan Poland, Lou Gentile, Jim Lime, Vic Delgado, and Lee Smith. Finally, I'm thankful to God for giving me a gift that I can share with the world.

KYB Consulting and Coaching

We help companies produce a quality product, efficiently and accident-free. Through training sessions and one-on-one coaching on the floor, we help plant management teams develop the skills and confidence they need to effectively lead the safety process and get employees working safely when they're not around.

For more information:
Call us at 331-457-9427 or
email us at kybcc.zic@gmail.com